WYLAM PAST

A Pictorial History of a Northumberland Village

Philip R.B. Brooks

Acknowledgements

I am most grateful to all those people who have kindly offered old photographs of Wylam, and encouraged my interest in the history of the village; without such help it would not have been possible to compile either my first book *Wylam – A History in Photographs* in 1995 or this second volume. The backing of subscribers and those who placed advance orders has ensured that adequate funding has been available to allow publication of this book to proceed without delay; thank you all. Special thanks to my wife, Barbara, for her support throughout; to the local libraries and archive offices for their assistance and to the staff of Bailes for their guidance during printing.

PHILIP R.B. BROOKS

The following have kindly permitted illustrations to be reproduced on the pages indicated:

Newcastle Libraries and Information Service (22, 24, 36, 49); National Railway Museum/Science and Society Picture Library (Front Cover); University of Newcastle upon Tyne (7, Back Cover); Science Museum, London/Science and Society Picture Library (34, 35); Newcastle Chronicle & Journal (45); Mrs A. Beresford (8); Miss D. Conley (37); Mrs C. Smith (31); the late E.E. Smith (2 5, 27, 43).

© Philip R.B. Brooks, 1998

Published by Philip R.B. Brooks, 20 Bluebell Close, Wylam, Northumberland NE41 8EU

ISBN: 0 9534090 0 7

All rights reserved. No part of this book may be reproduced, stored or introduced into a retrieval system, or transmitted in any form or by any means (electronic, mechanical, photocopying, recording or otherwise) without the prior permission of the publisher.

British Library Cataloguing in Publication data: a catalogue record for this book is available from the British Library.

Printed by. Bailes the Printer, Houghton le Spring

Front cover:

The River Wall at Wylam Scars 1836, by J.W. Carmichael. While the Newcastle and Carlisle Railway was still under construction, Newcastle publishers Messrs. Currie and Bowman commissioned one of Tyneside's finest artists, John Wilson Carmichael (1800-1868), to produce a unique series of drawings showing views along the line. This illustration was one of the earliest to be published and is dated 1836, the year after this first section of the railway, between Blaydon and Hexham had been opened. It shows the locomotive *Comet*, built by R. and W. Hawthorn in 1835 for £1,053 – hauling a train of assorted carriages and waggons eastwards towards Wylam Station. Those passengers who occupied seats on the roofs of the carriages were charged third-class fares, otherwise they were accommodated on seats or forms in open waggons; it was not until 1847 that third-class carriages were introduced. Wylam village lies on the north bank of the River Tyne, with the Haugh Pit on the extreme left; the ironworks and its blast furnace next and the bridge in the centre-right with its toll-house at the southern end. Further right is Wylam Station, now one of the oldest stations in the world still in regular use by passengers. Thanks to Carmichael and the publishers of the commemorative booklet in which his drawings first appeared in 1839, the Newcastle and Carlisle is probably better documented pictorially than any other of the early railways.

Other books by Philip Brooks:
Wylam and its Railway Pioneers (1975)
Where Railways were Born (1979)
William Hedley – Locomotive Pioneer (1980)
Wylam – A History in Photographs (1995)

Corrections needed in *Wylam – A History in Photographs*:
On Page 14:   The house shown under construction is No. 21 (not 24) Stephenson Terrace.
On Page 30:   The James family sold Holeyn Hall to Lt. Col. M.C. Woods in 1868 (not 1876).

Introduction

Those who have read my earlier book *Wylam – A History in Photographs* will recognise the following introduction. If, when I compiled that selection of old photographs for publication in 1995, I had known that I would be producing a second volume three years later I might have planned them with definite and different subjects in each (rather than as two assorted collections) and tailored the introductory text accordingly. However, the introduction below, which I wrote for the previous book, outlines the general history of the village and still seems just as appropriate as an introduction to the pictures in this second volume.

Wylam is situated on the banks of the River Tyne, midway between Newcastle upon Tyne and Hexham and two miles south of Hadrian's Wall. It lies within the District of Tynedale in the County of Northumberland.

The first references to the village occur shortly after the Norman Conquest when the manor of Wylam was in the possession of Tynemouth Priory. It had probably been given to the Priory by Guy de Baliol, Lord of Bywell at about the time of its foundation c.1085. The Prior subsequently established a house at Wylam where he occasionally held his Manor Court. The records of the Priory are contained in the Tynemouth Cartulary and give various details of the Prior's tenants in Wylam – their names, occupations, landholdings and duties – and references to coal working, milling and fishing.

Towards the end of the 13th Century the period of Scottish attacks on Northumberland began. In 1297, the year after the destruction of Hexham Priory, Wylam was 'laid waste' by the Scots under the command of William Wallace. Raids continued into the 14th century, and during one of these raids the Prior's House was destroyed and lay in ruins until it was rebuilt by the active Prior Whethamstead c.1405. Fragments of this early medieval house, which came to be known as the Sporting House, from its use by the Prior and monks for hunting and recreation, are incorporated in Wylam Hall. When Henry VIII began the suppression of the monasteries as part of the Reformation, between 1536-39, the period of 450 years during which Wylam had been in the possession of the Priors of Tynemouth came to an abrupt end.

If 1539 were the most significant landmark in Wylam's history during the 16th century, then 1679 was the local landmark in the 17th century when much of the land and property in the village was acquired by John Blackett of Horton Grange, near Ponteland; so beginning an unbroken period of almost 300 years until 1971, during which the Blackett family were Lords of the Manor of Wylam.

Little information on the size of the village exists prior to the official Government censuses which commenced in 1801 – but two returns survive listing those obliged to pay the Hearth Tax shortly before the Blacketts came to Wylam. In 1664, 9 people paid tax on property with one hearth and 14 people are recorded as too poor to pay. In 1675, 3 paid on property with two hearths, 5 with one hearth and 17 were too poor to pay. The earliest maps of the village to survive are from 1766 and 1770, both commissioned to show the extent of land and property owned by the Blacketts and one giving information about the state of the colliery. The collieries had been important in

"Colliery staithes on the Tyne"   *An 18th Century engraving*

Wylam's economy for centuries and during the mid 18th century the construction of the Wylam waggonway, one of the first in the North East, enabled coal to be transported between the colliery and staithes on the Tyne at Lemington and thence via keels to sea-going vessels at the mouth of the Tyne for export to London and elsewhere.

The last quarter of the 18th century saw the births locally of four individuals who were to be numbered among the world's most famous railway pioneers – William Hedley (1779), George Stephenson (1781) Timothy Hackworth (1786) and Nicholas Wood (1795). But it was after the arrival of Christopher Blackett as Lord of the Manor of Wylam in 1800, that the village became of world-wide significance in the development of the steam locomotive as a means of traction. By 1815 one or two locomotives such as that illustrated on the back cover of this book were hauling waggons back and forth along the 5 mile Wylam Waggonway. The diversification of Wylam's industries had begun in a modest way in 1799 with the establishment by Locke, Blackett and Co. of an ingenious, small lead-shot manufactory – using a disused mine-shaft, instead of building a tall shot-tower, but it was not until 1836 that a significant new industry – an ironworks – was founded. 1835/36 was remarkable for the opening of the first section of the Newcastle and Carlisle Railway between Blaydon and Hexham, along the south side of the Tyne the concurrent development of Wylam Ironworks on the north side and the construction by public subscription of the first bridge across the river, linking the ironworks and railway. One entrepreneur, Benjamin Thompson, was the key figure associated with all three projects which were of major significance for Wylam. His two sons ran the ironworks, manufacturing locomotives for various local railway and colliery companies, until the 1840s; they were succeeded by Bell Brothers, a firm who later moved to Teesside.

As a result of Wylam's industrial expansion, the population grew quite significantly during the first half of the 19th century;

J.F.B. Blackett, M.P.

from 673 in 1801, to 887 in 1831 and 1091 in 1851. From 1847-1856, J.F.B. Blackett served as village squire – one of the best educated and the most caring, who also became briefly an MP for Newcastle; sadly he died at the early age of 35. During his time the new British School was built (1854) and the village Reading Institution and News Room opened (1850). By the 1860s local industries were in decline with the closure of the ironworks in 1864 and of the main colliery, the Haugh Pit, in 1868. Although the loss of local employment resulted in a fall in population of almost 30% between 1861 and 1871, the decline could have resulted in more serious unemployment had the closure of the Haugh Pit not coincided with the opening of the West Wylam Colliery, a mile west of Wylam, where many miners and their families moved to live and work.

In the early 1870s following the rundown of local industries the village must have given a rather depressing appearance. Coincidentally, as part of a campaign to improve the conditions of miners and their families, the editor of the Newcastle Weekly Chronicle published a series of reports describing each of the pit villages in Northumberland and Durham. The description of Wylam, in the issue of 17 January 1874, was highly critical. However even if the pitmen's cottages were as squalid as was claimed, investment was being made elsewhere in the village during the 1870s. A new public railway was constructed on the north side of the river between Scotswood, Newburn and Wylam following the route of the former Wylam waggonway for much of its length, and linking with the Newcastle and Carlisle Railway at Scotswood to the east and Hagg Bank, just beyond Wylam to the west. North Wylam Station opened in 1875 and the line was completed in 1876. In the same year the Wesleyans built a new Chapel, and used their earlier Chapel of 1834 as an adjoining schoolroom. A few years before, in 1871, village miller Edward Milburn had been busy modernising his premises, converting them from water-power to steam-power.

Although pits at Wylam Hills (north-west of the farm), North Wylam (south-west of the Rift) and at the Hagg (south-west of Hagg Farm) continued to work periodically the village was no longer dominated by industry and became much more attractive as a place in which to live. By the 1880s good progress was being made in redeveloping many of the sites of the sub-standard cottages on the north side of the river and the new terraces of Ingham Row, Tyne View and West View were built near the bridge in what had been known as 'Wylam Engine' or 'Low Wylam' and the centre of the village in 'High Wylam', Burgoyne Terrace, Laburnum Terrace and Lishman's Cottages were completed. Several attractive individual stone houses were built during the 1880s and 90s, with the pleasant stone-fronted terraces of Stephenson, Falcon and Algernon following in the period to the First World War. However, the ready availability locally of red brick has meant that that has been widely used in houses on both sides of the river, sometimes where stone might have been preferable.

Thankfully stone was used for two important and prominent buildings in late Victorian times, the Parish Church of St Oswin of 1886 and the new Reading Room and Institute of 1896, both on Church Road. Similarly the Bird Inn and the Ship Inn on the Main Street were attractively re-built in stone. Although not in stone the new County Council Primary School of 1910 on Falcon Terrace, built on the site of the long-derelict ironworks was one of the early 20th Century improvements. Housing development between the wars was largely in the centre of the village along Woodcroft Road, Chapel Lane and Main Road, and on the north side along Holeyn Hall Road and Acomb Drive. Temporary guests during the Second World War were PoWs accommodated in Nissen huts on each side of Church Road above the Institute. Soon after the war the first local authority houses were built by Hexham RDC on Hedley Road, Hackworth Gardens and part of Jackson Road, and later on Bell Road and Parsons Road. More private housing followed when the former orchards at Florist Hall were developed with Woodvale Gardens and The Dene in the early 1960s. The largest development – the Dene Estate – followed in the late 1960s and 70s. These, and other smaller developments have meant that the village now has a total of some 850 dwellings and a population of almost 2,200.

Whilst many of the better-known photographs were included in my first book, I hope that the pictures which I have chosen in this second selection will be of equal interest. I have tried to make the captions as informative as possible, and have increased the size of print to make it easier to read. The two books which I have now compiled have used many of the old pictures of Wylam which have survived locally; however, I continue to search for more, and if any readers know of the existence of other pictures of the village, please contact me.

PHILIP R.B. BROOKS,
20 Bluebell Close,
Wylam

WYLAM. [By R. P. Leitch.]

Prepared by the artist R.P. Leitch for a new edition of Samuel Smiles biography of George and Robert Stephenson published in 1862, this is the earliest general view of Wylam from the east, whilst J.W. Carmichael's picture on the front cover is the oldest view from the west.

Leitch's engraving shows the bridge of 1836, with its stone piers and timber deck, in the centre; the Haugh Pit, with its winding gear on the left; the British School which opened in 1854, and is now the Wylam Assembly, can be seen in the centre background. Leitch seems to have used a little artistic licence in producing this illustration and not all the features shown are accurately positioned. The tower on the extreme right contained the pumping engine for the Engine Pit and was used for extracting water from the underground colliery workings; it was not, as had at one time been suggested, part of the ironworks which lay further east, and to the right of this view. Most of the groups of single-storey cottages, many with garret-bedrooms, were occupied by pitmen or ironworkers and their families. A salmon fisherman with his boat and nets is depicted in the foreground.

Between the late 1820's and early 1840's Tyneside artist Thomas H. Hair (1810-82) painted a series of views of collieries in Northumberland and Durham. These included two scenes at Wylam Colliery, one (reproduced on the back cover) depicting one of William Hedley's locomotive engines on the waggonway and the other (illustrated here) the Haugh Pit. In the foreground a locomotive stands with some twelve laden chaldron waggons alongside the Haugh Pit at the western extremity of the waggonway.

The Wylam locomotives were of 16 h.p. and able to haul up to 14 laden waggons, each holding just over two tons of coal, at a speed of about 5 miles per hour; it took one hour to travel the full length of the waggonway from the colliery at Wylam to the loading staithes at Lemington. On the left of this illustration is the colliery winding-engine house, with a small group of miners' cottages in the background; the pit shaft was on the south side of the waggonway, just to the right of the single waggon in the centre of the picture. The colliery closed in 1868 and the only visible reminder today is the tree-covered spoil heap alongside the River Tyne.

A Perspective View of Wylam House and Gardens – this engraving is the oldest surviving illustration of any building in Wylam, and was made in 1770 by Tyneside engraver Ralph Beilby (1743-1817).

He was commissioned by John Blackett IV (1735-1791) who had inherited the family estate in Wylam following the death of his father (John III) in 1769. Ralph Beilby prepared this engraving from a drawing by his elder brother William (1740-1819). The original copper plate from which the engraving was produced still exists. Beilby also prepared a companion engraving for John Blackett, described as *A Plan of the Wylam Estate, with the state of the colliery.* The Beilby account books have been preserved and an entry dated June 15th 1770 shows that he charged John Blackett 5 guineas (£5.25) for engraving each of the two copper plates, 12 shillings (60p) for four quires of paper and 12 shillings (60p) for making 200 impressions (presumably 100 from each engraved plate).

The main southern elevation of the House (later known as the Hall) remained largely unaltered from 1770 until the 1880's when banker Richard Clayton, who leased the property, built an extension to the west of the original house. A new northern wing was added in 1912-13 by Colonel E.U. Blackett. The photograph on the facing page shows the Hall prior to the fire of 1964.

A view of Wylam Hall from the east in 1963, soon after it had been sold by the Blackett family, having been in their ownership since about 1679. Parts of the Hall date back to medieval times, when the village was owned by the Priory at Tynemouth, and used as a 'Sporting House' or country retreat by the Benedictine monks. It was destroyed by the Scots during a raid on Wylam in 1297 and left in ruins until 1405, when it was rebuilt by Prior Whethamstead. The central portion (gable end facing) and the southern wing (left) were the oldest parts of the Hall, and are depicted in Ralph Beilby's engraving of 1770 (shown on the facing page). The date of the later hipped-roof building on the right is uncertain but probably late 18th or early 19th century. This building was taken down in 1963/64 when a scheme to renovate and convert the Hall into flats was being carried out by the new owners. Sadly a major fire on 24 September 1964, when conversion was almost complete, necessitated the demolition of the former southern wing (left) with its distinctive oval window. A subsequent conversion scheme was carried out to create four flats within the remaining part of the Hall.

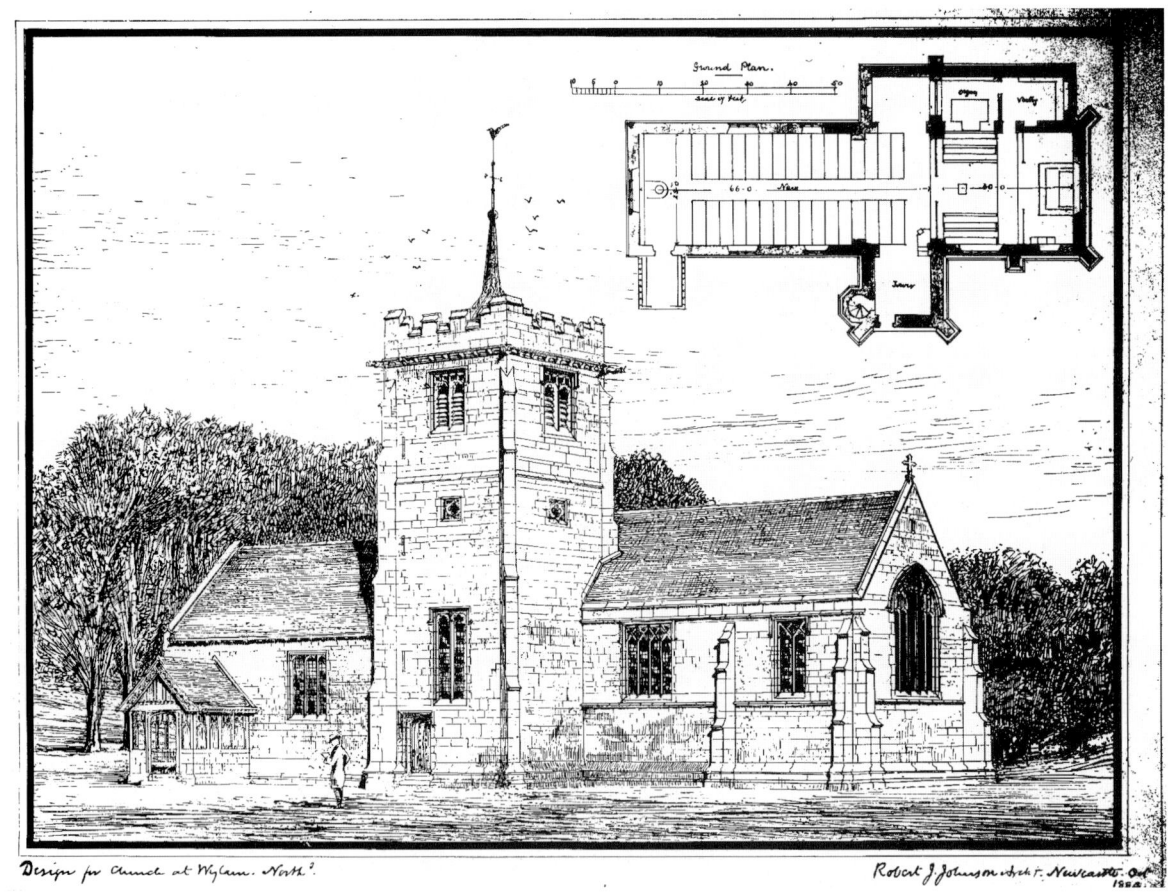

Before completion of the Parish Church of St Oswin in 1886, residents of Wylam who were Anglicans had to make the four-mile return journey to the Parish Church at Ovingham. In 1884 a fund had been launched to provide an Anglican Church in Wylam, the initial aim being to construct an iron church, which it was hoped would lead to the building of a permanent church and the creation of a separate parish of Wylam. Richard and Emily Clayton who lived at Wylam Hall were leading figures in this campaign and approached George Hedley, one of the wealthy coal-owner sons of the famous locomotive pioneer and former manager of Wylam Colliery, William Hedley and his wife Frances. George Hedley, who had been born in Wylam and spent his childhood in the village, immediately offered to build a fine church as a lasting memorial to his parents. A site was agreed and a distinguished Tyneside architect Robert J. Johnson chosen to design the new church. This drawing dated October 1884 shows an early design which was later slightly modified. The foundation stone was laid on 1 January 1885 by Mrs Clayton and the church dedicated on 1 November 1886. It cost just over £7,000. George's younger brother, William, subsequently built the Vicarage in 1888 and endowed the church.

All in their Sunday-best, although wearing a variety of different styles in the suits, shirts and hats, St Oswin's Church bellringers photographed at York Minster, but whether to receive an award or take part in a competition, we don't know. However we do have the names of most of those in the group. In the back row (standing from left to right), the tweed-suited bell-master Robert (?) Routledge; Rev. William S. Lloyd, popular Chaplain of St Oswin's from 1892 until 1902 when the first Vicar, Rev. H.H. Barff was installed; Ted Weightman; unidentified. Front row (left to right), Harry Wilkinson; Adam Pigg; Tom Weightman; Billy May; Andrew Dodd; Bob Vest. The presence of Rev. Lloyd, who moved to Ashington in 1902, dates this photograph as probably 1900-01. An enthusiastic team of bell-ringers had been formed soon after St Oswin's had been completed in 1886, and they first achieved their ambition to ring 740 changes – the greatest number that can be rung on a peal of six bells, in 1894.

Following the death of village miller Edward Milburn in October 1900, his nephew Edward (Ned) Young, who benefited from his uncle's will, took over the milling business. He obtained permission in July 1901 to build a large new house, 'Tyne Holme' (now known as 'River House') on the vacant site at the bridge end, which had been created a few years earlier by the demolition of a group of more than twenty dilapidated cottages known as 'The Square'. Although the plans for the new miller's house do not give the name of the architect, it is likely to have been William Bedlington, who designed the bridge toll-house and the new houses being built nearby at Stephenson Terrace. Stonemasons with their aprons and mallets are prominent in this photograph of the workmen employed in building Mr Young's new house in 1901/02. The detached coach-house and stables were completed the following year.

A quick glance at this photograph of about 1905 would suggest that little has changed in the past ninety years or so. In fact it is the only picture discovered showing (on the extreme right) the large warehouse which stood on the north side of the Scotswood, Newburn and Wylam Railway and just to the east of the site of Wylam Ironworks. It is thought that this three-storey building was part of the ironworks, which had been established in 1836 by Benjamin Thompson. Thompson had also surveyed the route for the Newcastle and Carlisle Railway and became one of the Railway Company directors, as well as promoting the scheme to build Wylam Bridge. His two sons were managing partners in the ironworks known as Thompson Brothers and they built locomotives for various companies including several for the Newcastle and Carlisle Railway. Bell Brothers acquired the works in August 1844 and expanded the range of products, but no longer built locomotives. The warehouse was demolished in 1906/07 when construction of the roadway and houses on Falcon Terrace commenced. The bridge toll-house and the miller's house (extreme left) were newly built at this date (see facing page).

It is rare for amateur photographers to mark their prints with the date when the photograph was taken. Fortunately the (unknown) photographer of this picture of the riverside at Wylam did so – it was 30th September 1908, and shows construction of the houses in Stephenson Terrace and Falcon Terrace (in the background) half completed. William Bedlington was the architect and William Strachan of Haltwhistle the builder of most of the houses in Stephenson Terrace. Henry Wallace and Sons of Hexham built those in Falcon Terrace. Numbers 1-10 and 17-23 Stephenson Terrace are completed and occupied at this date; in the background, and seen through the gap between Numbers 10-17 Stephenson Terrace, are Numbers 10-14 Falcon Terrace, although Numbers 1-9 had not yet been built. However the eastern half of Falcon Terrace (Numbers 15-29) was already completed, and some of these houses can be seen on the extreme right. The houses in Stephenson Terrace replaced dilapidated miners cottages known as East Water Row, which had been demolished by 1895.

General View, Wylam. 2032

One of the many postcards of local scenes published by the prolific firm of Robert Johnston and Sons of Gateshead. They had 14,500 negatives of views of every town and village in the four Northern Counties and printed half-a-million postcards each year. Their cards provide a very valuable photographic record of many communities during the first half of the twentieth century. Sadly their works in West Street, Gateshead, holding extensive stocks of negatives and cards were destroyed in a disastrous fire on 18 January 1946.

Much of this view is now obscured by the trees which have grown up on both sides of the river. There is no longer any ground on the riverside below the station where cattle could safely graze. Little obvious change has taken place to the buildings in this view since the photograph was taken in 1912, except for the mill chimney (centre left background) which was demolished following the fire which destroyed the mill in August 1931 (See page 21).

The unveiling of the village war memorial on Saturday 10th March 1923 more than four years after the end of the First World War, was a sad but memorable occasion. It received wide coverage in local newspapers, and several of the photographs taken were sold afterwards as commemorative postcards. By chance this picture is the only one found which shows the last Lord of the Manor of Wylam, Christopher J.W. Blackett (second left) at a public event – and probably his first – within the village. A few minutes after this photograph was taken he unveiled the memorial. The others in this picture who all spoke during the ceremony are: Colonel E.P.A. Riddell (left), Rev. G. Mills, the local Wesleyan Minister between 1918-1923 and (right) Rev. H.H. Barff, the first Vicar of Wylam who served from 1902-1929. C.J.W. Blackett was the only son of Colonel Edward Umfreville Blackett and his second wife Sybell. He inherited the family estate in Wylam on reaching the age of 21 in 1921, following the death of his father the previous year. A shy but kind and generous bachelor he died in 1971, the last male member of the family who had served as Lords of the Manor of Wylam for almost 300 years.

Another photograph taken at the unveiling of the village war memorial in 1923. Those in this picture include (left to right) Charles Atkinson of West House, who was Secretary of the War Memorial Committee; Sir Charles Parsons of Holeyn Hall, whose only son was killed at Ypres in 1918; Richard Taylor of Rose Cottage and in the long overcoat, John Lishman of South Hill, the Chairman of the Parish Council. Others identified in the centre background include Sir James Knott of Close House, who lost two sons in the War (see page 31); F. Stirling Newall of Castle Hill; Edward Young of Tyne Holme, a local councillor and the village miller; Ralph Brady, the schoolmaster; John Charlton of Loughrigg, a church-warden at St Oswin's for 26 years, and Mr Matthews, the village postman. The elegant memorial was designed by architects W. Dixon and Son of Newcastle. The names of the forty-two men killed in the First World War and later the eleven killed in the Second World War are recorded on the bronze panels. The railings – which enclosed the memorial were taken for scrap during one of the 'Feed the Guns' campaigns in the Second World War.

No trace of this house survives today – and nothing on this photograph would give anyone a clue as to where it stood. However, the picture was in the family album of Mr Harry Shipley of Horsley, and is the house where his mother, Lucy, was born; she is the little girl standing by the door with her parents George and Annie Weightman. Known as Cross House, and later as Ivy House, it was situated on what is now the War Memorial green, facing west up the village, and with a view from the back looking eastwards across the North Wylam Station Yard. It almost certainly dates from the mid-18th century, but we know nothing of its early history. This photograph was taken in 1893/94 shortly before the house and the rows of pitmen's cottages which stood nearby in Waggonway Row and East Water Row were all demolished and replaced by the more elegant houses in Stephenson Terrace. George Weightman was a traveller for Wylam Mill and his wife Annie was a niece of Edward Milburn the local miller. They had come to Wylam in 1870 and Lucy was the youngest of their six children.

Wylam's version of artist John Constable's painting *The Haywain*. A tranquil scene of a farm waggon laden with hay, with two horses and a cartman – all posing patiently for the photographer in front of Ingham Row. A cart can also be seen on the left outside Wylam Mill. Allowing ivy or virginia creeper to cover the front of your house appears to have been the fashion in the 1920's, and all the houses in Ingham Row (built in 1891) are similarly camouflaged. It would be hazardous today to park in this position, but the pace of life, and of traffic, was much more leisurely when this picture was taken. This was one of the series of postcards of Wylam published by W.H. Smith, Sons and Nephew in the early years of the century when sending postcards was fashionable and millions were sold and sent in the U.K. each year.

A corn watermill is recorded in the village towards the end of the 11th century when the Manor of Wylam came into the possession of Tynemouth Priory. The four-storey mill building shown in this photograph of c.1906 dominated Low Wylam from the 18th century and perhaps earlier, until 1931 when it was destroyed in a spectacular fire (see facing page). The building on the left was the miller's house until 1902 when a new house (see pages 12 and 13) was built and the old house became the mill offices. The 1851 census lists John Brown (44) as village miller, his wife Ann (32) and a baby son; Edward Milburn (26) was described as a 'miller's servant'. Later that year John Brown died and his wife then ran the mill for several years with Edward Milburn as manager. At that time the mill had a water-wheel and three pairs of grind-stones. In 1865 Ann Brown died and Milburn took over the mill. He converted it from water-power to steam-power in 1871 and undertook other improvements, including building the mill stables (now Wylam Garage Showroom). On Milburn's death in 1900 a nephew Ned Young continued the business, and he is seen in this picture of c.1905 standing in the doorway of the mill, behind the cart.

The front gable wall of Wylam Mill as it appeared on the morning of 9th August 1931; the firemen from Newburn with their elegant helmets, still damping down the burning embers following the disastrous fire which gutted the mill premises the previous night. Compare this picture with that on the facing page showing the same view of the mill entrance some 25 years earlier. One of the abiding memories of residents of the houses in Ingham Row, who lived directly opposite the mill and watched the fire, was of dozens of rats fleeing from the burning mill and running down to the river. All the old mill buildings, including the tall chimney which had been a prominent local landmark, were subsequently demolished. The owners, T.G. Dyke and Son, who also had grocery stores at Throckley and Horsley, rebuilt the Wylam Mill premises in 1933. It continued in use as a mill until 1948, when it was used briefly as a bottling factory by Rodford and Peel; by 1950 it was a bakery and was acquired by Laws Stores in 1953. In 1983 the business closed and the following year the building was converted into flats.

An attractive rural scene showing the farmhouse at Bradley Mill Farm in the early 1890's. The farm and the adjoining watermill were traditionally part of the Bradley Hall Estate owned by the Simpson family from the early 17th century and which passed to the Liddell family in 1844. The Hall was occupied by John Walker of Seaton Burn at the time of the 1851 census and he later purchased the estate. In 1853 William Johnson was the tenant of Bradley Mill Farm which then comprised the farmhouse, the corn mill and 37 acres of land. In January 1857 Robert Marshall leased the farm and the watermill for £60 p.a., and continued to live and work there as a miller and flour dealer until the early 1890's. Ownership changed in November 1869 when C.J. Cruddas acquired the farm and the mill together with Wylam Wood Farm, which had also been part of the Bradley Hall Estate. In 1896, a few years after this photograph was taken, Cruddas obtained permission to alter and extended the farmhouse and this work was probably done after the Marshalls had left. Although the appearance of the farmhouse has changed, the snaking line of the road to Crawcrook and the presence of the Stanley burn in the foreground make this scene recognisable today.

The ford at Bradley Mill where the Stanley burn flowed across Station Road was always an attraction for children, and was popularly known as 'The Splash'. This photograph of about 1904 looks westwards and is one of several taken by Thomas Waller who lived with his family at 'Rushmere', Elm Bank Road between 1902 and 1920. The small boy in the foreground, resplendent in sailor-suit is his son Jack and the man with the bicycle is the village postman. The house amongst the trees is 'Stanley Vale', the first new house to be built in South Wylam, and described in the 1881 census return as 'Mr Cooke's new house'. George Cooke was born at Ryton about 1821, and by 1841 was living at Wylam Hills and working as a gardener. He was employed by wealthy Tyneside lead-merchant Edward James at Wylam Hall. When James built Holeyn Hall in 1853 the Cooke family moved to the gardener's house there. His wife, Sarah, died in 1878 and by 1881 George Cooke had built and was living in 'Stanley Villa' (later renamed 'Stanley Vale'), a distinctive brick house with a partially walled garden; he remained there until his death in 1900. Station Road was re-aligned, and a bridge built across the Stanley burn in 1972 to eliminate the ford and speed traffic!

The elegant bridge which carried the Scotswood, Newburn and Wylam Railway over the River Tyne at 'The Hagg' west of Wylam, shown under construction in 1876. This view looking north-east is one of several photographs almost certainly taken for W.G. Laws, the engineer who designed the bridge and who subsequently became City Engineer of Newcastle upon Tyne. The suspended platform deck of this single-span 240ft. long wrought iron bridge is only three feet above the height to which the Tyne had risen in a tremendous flood in 1771 when all the bridges across the river were destroyed except that at Corbridge. Because of fears that work involved in building piers might penetrate the shallow underground workings of the local collieries which extended under the river in this vicinity and cause flooding, the bridge was designed as a single span, avoiding piers. The main contractor was W.E. Jackson and Co. of Newcastle upon Tyne, with Hawks and Crawshay of Gateshead supplying the ironwork. Completed at a cost of £16,000 the bridge was opened on 6th October 1876. Now preserved as a distinctive footbridge, it was given a major refurbishment in 1997.

A short train of four coaches being hauled by Gresley Class V1 2-6-2T locomotive No. 67687 (based at the BR depot at Blaydon) from the North Wylam branch across the 'Points' bridge onto the Newcastle and Carlisle line in the mid 1950's. When the railway between Scotswood, Newburn and Wylam was being planned along the north bank of the River Tyne in the early 1870's, the importance of constructing a bridge across the river (see facing page) to provide a link with the North Eastern Railway west of Wylam was emphasised since at that time the collieries at Heddon, Throckley and Walbottle were sending large quantities of coal and coke to Carlisle and West Cumberland. However, comparatively little use was ever made of the North Wylam branch for through-passenger services over the new bridge, which was mainly used by goods trains and special excursions, or on those occasions when the Newcastle-Carlisle line south of the Tyne was closed for repair. In the background of this photograph the plantation of trees to the right of the bridge covers the disused spoil heap of the former Haugh Pit at Wylam Colliery.

Built overlooking the Newcastle and Carlisle Railway west of its junction with the Scotswood, Newburn and Wylam line and just east of where the sidings led into the West Wylam Colliery (see facing page), the hamlet of Hagg Bank has traditionally been known locally as 'The Points' – although no points exist today. The first terrace of four houses was built by the North Eastern Railway Company for their employees c.1880. At the time of the 1881 census the occupants were two signalmen and two porters with their families. In 1890/91 one of the signalmen, Robert Turnbull, together with George Lamb, the main local provision merchant who lived at Laburnum House on the Main Street in Wylam, built the first eight houses in Front Street (on the left of this photograph). All the houses in Hagg Bank were completed during the 1880's and 1890's and remarkably little has changed since this picture was taken almost a century ago. The ready availability of cheap bricks from the nearby brickworks at West Wylam Colliery helped reduce the price of most of these houses when built – it is said – to little more than £50.

One of the fine local railway photographs taken in the 1950's by the late E.E. Smith. This view (c.1953) from just west of the road bridge leading to the hamlet of Hagg Bank looks north-west towards Ovingham in the distance and shows a well-laden goods train travelling east. The siding to the left served the collieries and brickworks at West Wylam until shortly before the last pit closed in 1960. The two trackside buildings were built by the Newcastle and Carlisle Railway Company as cottages for their employees. Mr Robert Turnbull, an NER signalman, and his family occupied the cottage in the foreground in the 1870's before he moved to one of the new NER cottages built in Hagg Bank c.1880 (see facing page). Not used as cottages since at least the 1920's these two buildings were demolished in the early 1970's. This length of the Newcastle and Carlisle Railway at Hagg Bank was where construction work started at the eastern end of the line in February 1831. When the route for the railway was initially planned it had been intended to dig a tunnel at Hagg Bank, but by a general raising of the level of the line, this was avoided and a cutting excavated instead – a much cheaper solution.

Wylam has been well served by its doctors – at least since early Victorian times. John Ismay Atkinson (left), whose father was a glass manufacturer at Heworth, near Sunderland, came as village doctor in 1839 at the age of 23, and was still working in Wylam when he died forty-four years later. Soon after arrival he moved into West House, Ovingham Road and initially lived there with his sister, Elizabeth, until his marriage to Hannah Armstrong (right), daughter of a local land agent, at St Andrew's Parish Church, Heddon-on-the-Wall, on 12 September 1848. Shortly after starting his practice in Wylam he submitted evidence to a Royal Commission investigating the employment of children in collieries, lead mines and ironworks. The Commission report of 1842 provides descriptions of the working conditions experienced by children employed in local industries at that time. He served as colliery surgeon to several colliery companies and took an active part in village life. Dr Atkinson died in 1883 and his wife in 1908. Two of their children, Jennie and Charles did not marry and continued to live at West House until Charles died in 1949.

Elegant Edwardian ladies wearing a wide variety of fashions at a 'Sale of Work' held in the detached garden of Dr and Mrs Atkinson's family home, West House, in about 1908. The garden was on the south side of Ovingham Road, and the neighbouring house, in the background of this picture, is 'Wylam Lodge', which was built in 1877 by Mrs Sarah Kell. West House, on the north side of Ovingham Road (and off to the right of this picture) dates back at least to the 17th century. In 1783 the house was described as 'known by the sign of the Bay Horse' and later that year was sold by auction to a brewer, J. Thompson. Early in the 1800's it was one of several properties in the village owned by William Brown. These included Wylam Brewery, situated further east along the Ovingham Road on the site now occupied by Blackett Court flats. By the 1830's his great grandson had sold the family property in Wylam, including the brewery, and it seems likely that West House had reverted back from an inn to a dwelling house by this date. Village doctor, Dr J.I. Atkinson, moved to Wylam in 1839 and was living in West House by 1841 (see facing page). Members of his family lived there for more than a century.

Although Close House dates from 1779 the site has been occupied since the 13th century, and perhaps earlier. For part of the early period the estate was owned by the Read family, but in about 1624 it was sold to Robert Bewicke, a Merchant Adventurer who had been Sheriff of Newcastle in 1615 and became Mayor in 1628 and 1637. It remained in the ownership of the Bewicke family until 1958. The mansion house and 151 acres of parkland and playing fields were acquired in 1961 by the University of Newcastle upon Tyne for £19,500 'as a major Sports Centre for outdoor exercise, for which space was not available within the city'. The present Close House was built in 1779 for Calverly and Mary Bewicke and although the name of the architect is unrecorded it is very like work undertaken elsewhere by William Newton, whose buildings in Northumberland include Backworth Hall, Dinnington Hall, Whitfield Hall and the Assembly Rooms in Newcastle upon Tyne. Before its acquisition by the University the best-known private resident of Close House this century was wealthy steamship and colliery owner Sir James Knott. He leased the estate in 1906 and continued to live there until a few years ago before his death in 1935 (see also facing page). This photograph dates from about 1900.

Sir James Knott, extreme right, poses with a group of workmen relaying roads on the Close House Estate, probably in the early 1920's. Born at Howdon on Tyne in 1855, James Knott founded the *Prince* line of steamships and became the largest shipowner in the North-East. He moved to Close House, Wylam in 1906. Tragedy hit the family during the First World War when two of the three sons were killed. The youngest, Captain Henry Basil Knott, fell at Ypres in September 1915, aged 24, and in July 1916 the second son, Major James Leadbitter Knott DSO, was killed on the Somme, aged 33. The eldest son survived the war in a Prisoner of War Camp after serving in Gallipoli and Palestine. After the death of his second son, Knott sold his fleet of steamships and retired from business and public affairs; he was created a baronet in July 1917. He built the tower of St George's Church, Ypres, and the Church of St James and St Basil, Fenham, in memory of his two sons. Sir James was a generous benefactor to numerous causes during his lifetime and a charitable trust bearing his name, continues to help and support many community projects in the North East.

The history of Oakwood House has yet to be researched but the earliest surviving detailed map of Wylam, dating from 1766, shows the house and almost 90 acres of surrounding farmland and woodland to the north of the village, as being in the ownership of Robert Sparrow. However by 1793 Thomas Blackett, who had become Lord of the Manor of Wylam two years earlier, was living at Oakwood. The house continued to be used occasionally by members of the Blackett family but the longest and most notable occupiers were a branch of the Cookson family – prominent Tyneside industrialists with business interests in lead, glass and chemicals. Norman C. Cookson who became Chairman of the Cookson Lead Company leased the Oakwood Estate from E.U. Blackett in 1877 at £255 per year. The lease was renewed for a further 21 years in 1889 when Cookson agreed to undertake various improvements to the house and to replace Oxclose Cottages on Blue Bell Lane with a terrace of four houses (the present Oakwood Cottages). He also built the lodge at the north entrance to the estate on the Heddon-Horsley road. Members of the Cookson family were generous local benefactors, notably towards the cost of the new Institute built in 1896. N.C. Cookson died in 1909, but his widow, Phoebe, remained at Oakwood until 1923. Her brother, Frederick Stirling Newall and his family lived at Castle Hill (see facing page).

Castle Hill House, situated south of Wylam on the road to Crawcrook, was designed and built in 1878-79 by Tyneside architect Archibald M. Dunn as his own family residence. Born in 1832, A.M. Dunn trained as an architect in the office of Charles Hansom of Bristol, before returning to Tyneside. The Dunn family had been staunch Roman Catholics for generations, and many of the Catholic churches and schools built in Northumberland and Durham during the second half of the 19th century were designed by A.M. Dunn or one of his partners. In Newcastle these included the impressive tower of St. Mary's Cathedral, St Dominic's Church on New Bridge Street, Neville Hall (the Mining Institute) and the former College of Medicine on Northumberland Road. He almost certainly designed Prudhoe Hall and the Catholic Church and school in Prudhoe – all for wealthy Catholic coal-owner Matthew Liddell. In about 1900 Dunn sold Castle Hill to the Gateshead industrialist F. Stirling Newall and moved to Bournemouth where he died in 1917. Following the deaths of Mr and Mrs Stirling Newall in the early 1930's, their son Geoffrey presented Castle Hill to the Royal Victoria Infirmary in 1933, in memory of his parents.

Puffing Billy is one of the original Wylam locomotives of 1813 designed by William Hedley, the colliery manager, and built at Wylam with assistance from blacksmith Timothy Hackworth and enginewright Jonathan Forster. It worked on the 5 mile waggonway hauling chaldron waggons between Wylam Colliery and the river staithes at Lemington, where the coal was transferred to keels, for transport to seagoing vessels at the mouth of the Tyne. This photograph was taken at the Haugh Pit in the early 1860s and shows *Puffing Billy* with the driver J. Carr (right) and fireman W. Greener (left). In the background are three buildings still standing today – the former school of 1854 (far left), Laburnum House (centre) and the Wesleyan Chapel of 1834 (before extension in 1876) on the extreme right. In 1862 *Puffing Billy* was taken to London for an exhibition associated with the new Patent Office (now Science) Museum, and was subsequently purchased by the Patent Office for £200 – a price which the owner, Captain E.A. Blackett, thought quite inadequate!

Wylam Dilly was used on the colliery waggonway for some 50 years. Built c.1813-15 to the general design of William Hedley, the viewer (manager) at Wylam Colliery it remained at Wylam until the colliery closed in October 1868, and was included among the colliery equipment sold by auction early in 1869. In his sale catalogue E.U. Blackett noted that the engine sold for just £16-10-0 (£16.50) which shows that it was probably in scrap condition. It was purchased at the auction, or shortly afterwards by William Hedley's sons, who later restored and displayed it at Craghead, one of the Hedley family collieries, near Stanley, Durham. This photograph was taken at Craghead Colliery c.1880; standing on the left are William and George Hedley; on the locomotive are the fireman William Robson and the engineman William Smith; in the background on the right is probably Mr T. Bell, Inspector of Mines for Durham. After display at the North East Coast Exhibition at Tynemouth in 1882 *Wylam Dilly* was transferred to the Royal Scottish Museum in Edinburgh; with *Puffing Billy* already at the Science Museum (see facing page), this ensured that two of William Hedley's historic early Wylam locomotives were preserved.

The neglected appearance of Stephenson's Cottage in this photograph of 1890 confirms that little attempt can have been made to renovate it for the Centenary of George Stephenson's birth in 1881, less than ten years' earlier. When George was born there on 9th June 1781 the Stephenson family occupied the downstairs room to the left of the doorway; other families lived in each of the three remaining rooms; access to the upper rooms was by an internal ladder. The Scotswood, Newburn and Wylam Railway, the public railway that replaced the 18th century waggonway which ran past the front of the cottage, was completed in 1876. The availability of this new public railway enabled the birthplace to become an important feature in the 1881 celebrations and on the actual centenary a special train carried many prominent individuals from Newcastle Central Station to North Wylam. The train stopped outside the cottage, where they paid homage to Stephenson, and the Mayor of Newcastle upon Tyne planted an oak tree (which is still growing) in the field behind the cottage. The special train then continued to North Wylam Station where sixteen modern locomotives loaned by the major railway companies were displayed. Sadly no photographs taken of the Centenary ceremonies at Wylam have yet been found.

"Under a spreading chestnut tree, the village smithy stands " – so wrote the 19th century poet Henry Longfellow – but not about Wylam! Among the colliery workshops and behind the corn mill would have been a more accurate description of the position of Wylam's blacksmith's forge. Taken in the late 1890's this photograph shows bearded blacksmith Ralph Henderson (centre) with son Jack (left) and an unidentified customer (right) – perhaps a local farmer or tradesman, standing outside the forge. Ralph Henderson moved his family from Byker Hill to Wylam in 1879, to set up as village blacksmith, probably succeeding George Cowens who had been the local blacksmith for forty years. Two of Jack Henderson's sons, John and Stanley, joined the family business, becoming motor engineers and electricians as demand for traditional blacksmithing diminished. The forge building was almost certainly originally part of the workshop where the famous Wylam Colliery locomotives *Puffing Billy* and *Wylam Dilly* (see pages 34 and 35) were repaired and maintained.

'Tynedale' and 'Riversdale', the substantial pair of semi-detached houses in the centre of this view at what is now the western end of Woodcroft Road, were built c.1900 to designs by architect William Bedlington. From 1902 'Riversdale' was occupied by Dr W.H. Bishop who had moved into Wylam as one of the village doctors in 1895, and it has continued to be used as a surgery by successors in the medical practice which he established. The attractive landscaped gardens on the left of this photograph belong to the house 'Prizedale' (later renamed 'Priorsdale') which was built in 1888 for market gardener Matthew Maughan and his wife and also designed by William Bedlington. The Maughan's cultivated the Florist Hall nurseries in the village and the name 'Prizedale' is reputed to reflect the fact that they grew prize dahlias! Less attractive in the background on the left is the gaunt boarded-up shell of the cottage which had served as the first Reading Institution and News Room from 1850 to 1896. Further to the right is the former British school, with Burgoyne Terrace alongside and the new Institute and the Parish Church behind.

Cultivating allotments was clearly a more popular pastime in 1926 when this photograph was taken, showing well-tended plots, than it is today when many of these riverside allotments are vacant and overgrown. The few large stone houses built at the western end of the road before the First World War (see facing page) were followed by more modest houses during the 1920's and 30's no doubt in part reflecting the years of economic uncertainty which many people faced in the unsettled inter-war period. At least three different builders, A. Pigg and Son, and J.R. Waugh of Wylam, and Hunters of Throckley, were involved in building on Woodcroft Road during this period. The unmade track leading down across the 'Bumble Box' bridge over the railway to the riverside allotments marked the end of development at this date. Building on the land further east had not yet commenced but would continue in the late 1920's and 30's. The name 'Woodcroft' was chosen because ancestors of the Blackett family of Wylam had owned the Manor of Woodcroft near Stanhope in County Durham during the 14th century.

Another of those tantalising photographs about which very little is known! A splendid group of football players, officials and supporters proud enough to display a massive 'Wylam' banner, and certainly a picture for the album – with everyone smartly dressed. From the style of clothing, and a few identifiable faces among the group, it certainly dates from the period just before the First World War, but the occasion (which league competition or what cup had they won?) – is lost in the mists of time unless anyone can supply more information? Although the rising ground behind the goal looks very much like the west end of what is now the village playing field, with the disused tree-covered spoil heap of the former Haugh Pit in the background, this field was used by the local butcher for grazing livestock and is not thought to have been in use as a playing field until the 1920's. If it is not Wylam – where is it – and when?

A keen group of local men preparing to plant potatoes, as part of a 'Dig for Victory' campaign during the First World War. The site is allotment gardens on Chapel Lane, where the Masonic Hall was subsequently built in 1928. Most of the land bounded by the Main Road, Chapel Lane and Woodcroft Road was not developed until the late 1920's and 1930's, although Barclay's Bank and the West Wylam and Prudhoe Co-operative Society store (now the pharmacy) on the corner of Chapel Lane had been built in 1915. Most of those in this photograph have been identified (from left to right): Billy Smith, Jack Sheldrake, Bob Elliot, Tom Marley, Bob Nelson, Ned Weightman (bending), unidentified, Billy May and Alf Dixon. Their flat caps, shirts and waistcoats are all typical of the period. Clay pipes, such as that being smoked by Billy May were widely used by local working men until the 1930's.

The staff at North Wylam Station pose proudly – if solemnly – in front of the trellis archway, which was part of the attractive station garden. Edwin Stabler, on the extreme right, served as Station Master for more than twenty years into the early 1920's. He was a founder-member of the George Stephenson Lodge of Freemasons. This is one of several surviving photographs taken at North Wylam Station in about 1911. The partially-completed houses in Falcon Terrace can be seen in the background. The eastern section was started in late 1906/early 1907 and was completed by 1910. The two end houses (Nos. 13 and 14) in the western section are finished, but those further west have not yet been started. Most houses were built and occupied by 1912 although several in the western section were not completed until after the end of the First World War. The sign on the extreme left of the photograph confirms the builders as H. Wallace and Sons – Wylam and Hexham. Information on the names of the railway staff (other than Mr Stabler) in the photograph would be welcome.

A scene of mixed steam and diesel working at North Wylam Station in 1958 – the year in which Diesel Multiple Units (DMU) were introduced in the North-East. In this photograph by the late E.E. Smith, a Derby-built DMU stands alongside the signalbox whilst a V-class 2-6-2T locomotive waits tender – first with a goods van and several carriages at the other platform. The goods shed lies on the extreme left, with the yard crane and houses in Ingham Row in the background; the houses on the right are in Falcon Terrace. In the early 1950's the journey by train between Newcastle and North Wylam took 23 minutes, stopping at each of the five intermediate stations; the cheap day return fare was 1/4 (7p). The North Wylam line (originally the Scotswood, Newburn and Wylam Railway) closed to all passenger traffic and to all goods traffic west of Newburn on 11 March 1968. Following acquisition by Northumberland County Council, the station yard area in this picture was cleared in 1975 to create a car park, with a pleasant walkway extending along the former trackbed between Hagg Bank and Newburn.

Public houses were often amongst the most stylish buildings designed in the Victorian and Edwardian eras – and the Bird Inn and the adjoining Ship Inn (rebuilt 1904/05), in the centre of Wylam are good examples. The Bird Inn was rebuilt by its owners, the Newcastle Breweries in 1897/98, to designs by J. Oswald and Sons, an architectural practice who designed many pubs for Newcastle Breweries between 1855 and 1969. John Phillips was landlord of the Bird Inn from about 1880 until his death in January 1900, aged 50. His widow, Hannah, continued as landlady up to the late 1920's. The property on the right bears the initials and date EUB 1890 confirming that it was built by Edward Umfreville Blackett, Lord of the Manor of Wylam from 1873 to 1920. At the time of this photograph (c.1905) the draper's shop in the central portion of the building was occupied by 30-year-old John Davison. His great-grandmother Ann Davison had been a grocer and draper in the village in 1841 and following her death in 1868 her widowed daughter Elizabeth continued to run the business and also serve as Postmistress almost to the end of the century when grandson John succeeded her. The Post Office moved to its present position on the corner of Laburnum Terrace and Chapel Lane in about 1901/02 with Benjamin Reeves as Postmaster.

At the outbreak of the Second World War St Oswin's Parish Hall was requisitioned by the War Office. Initially British troops were billeted there, but later when a Prisoner of War Camp was established in the village Italian and subsequently German PoW's occupied the hall. Six Nissen huts were also erected on the Glebe field (where the house 'Stonecutters' now stands) and three on the opposite side of Church Road where the Police House is today (see page 48). The camp guard-room was situated close to the church. Volunteers prepared breakfast for the PoW's, many of whom were sent to work on local farms whenever they were needed. Some of the Italian PoW's were basket-makers by trade and used willows from the riverside to make baskets for village residents. One of the German PoW's in the Wylam camp was Bert Trautman who played as goalkeeper for the PoW's team in local football matches. After moving to the Manchester area his talent was spotted by Manchester City Football Club and he had a distinguished career with that club. The model Bavarian castle shown in this photograph was built by German PoW's on the west side of Church Road. Unfortunately it collapsed during attempts to lift it from the site, when the camp was cleared in 1948.

The earliest detailed illustration of Wylam Bridge is the engraving by R.P. Leitch c.1862 (see page 6) which clearly shows the timber struts supporting each span of the bridge. By the 1890's it was necessary to replace the timber decking; a narrower deck with steel girders and cast-iron railings was used. The form of construction can be seen on this photograph from the 1920's, as can the blocked holes in the stone piers, where the timber struts shown in Leitch's engraving had been fixed. The size of the stone piers suggests that the original bridge was wider than the 11 feet to which it was redecked in the 1890's. It remained at that width and with a weight restriction of 4 tons until 1942 when it was widened with a concrete deck to enable it to be used by military tanks with weights of up to 40 tons. Before this widening, and during the invasion threats at the beginning of the war, in the summer of 1940, the bridge was prepared for demolition, to help halt any possible German advance in the North-East. Army engineers almost cut through the bridge at both ends and arrangements were made to place explosive charges there. The route of the old ford road - the only means of crossing the river before the bridge was built in 1836 - can be seen in the background on the right.

The opening of the first section of the Newcastle and Carlisle Railway, construction of Wylam Ironworks and the completion of the bridge across the river were three major events which all took place within twelve months in 1835/36. Although the bridge eased communications, the fact that it and the neighbouring bridges at Newburn and Ovingham were all toll bridges was a constant source of resentment when most other bridges elsewhere in the county were free. The fact that the residents of the more expensive houses in South Wylam also had free passes, thanks to a deal negotiated with the Bridge Company by a previous landowner, only increased local bitterness! However pressure from the Parish Council and residents over many years eventually resulted in the County Council purchasing the bridge, the toll house and part of the access road for £7,249 in 1936. A formal ceremony to free the bridge from tolls took place on 2 December 1936, and this photograph shows local residents crossing the bridge after a ceremonial ribbon had been cut by Mrs Whitelaw, the wife of local County Councillor Robert R. Whitelaw. Among those in the front who have been identified (from the left) are Thomas Pattinson, Ernest Reeve, Robert Whitelaw, Bob Henderson, Mrs Whitelaw, Dick Taylor, Jack Wright, Bob Wilkinson (?) and Jo Lee.

An aerial view of Wylam in 1947, looking east. In the centre foreground Ovingham Road leads into Main Road which sweeps through the centre of the village to the bridge over the Tyne, in the top right corner. The trees in the bottom left corner are within the grounds of Wylam Hall. Above this is the Parish Church, with the groups of Nissen huts of the Prisoner of War Camp on each side of Church Road (see page 45). East of the Institute garden is the row of cottages in the Ship Inn yard, since demolished to create the car park. On the opposite corner, where Blackett Court flats now stand, are several of the original buildings of the old brewery, behind Brewery House. In the centre-left the orchards and market gardens surrounding Florist Hall can be seen; developed in the 1960's with houses in Woodvale Gardens and the Dene. The white houses are the first built by Hexham RDC in Hedley Road and Hackworth Gardens. Further houses were built on the land to the east in 1957, while the fields to the left (north) were developed as the Dene Estate by Greensitt and Barratt in the late 1960's and early 1970's. The North Wylam branch line railway runs from top centre to the bottom right corner of this photograph.

Another aerial view, looking north, and taken in September 1948 only one year after that on the facing page. Holeyn Hall, former home of Sir Charles Parsons the turbine engineer, lies in the top right corner. In the opposite (top left) corner, Horsley Wood extends to the north west of Howdene Burn, the boundary between the parishes of Wylam and Horsley. In the central band of the picture Wylam Hall stands on the left; part of the grounds were developed with The Orchard in the 1970's. To the right are the Institute and the Parish Church. The Nissen huts and the PoW camp shown in the picture on the facing page had been cleared early in 1948. The orchards of Florist Hall and the fields to the north-east remained undeveloped until the 1960's when the houses in Woodvale Gardens and the Dene Estate were built. Along the north bank of the river the allotments occupy the haughland to the west of the old pit-heap, covered with trees, whilst the playing field lies to the east. A row of pipes lie waiting to be laid along the top of the field parallel with the railway cutting. The sandy beach along the riverbank is much more extensive than it is today.

Harry MacDowell, with his wooden leg, was a well-known local character who lived in the former toll-keepers cottage at Holeyn Hall crossroads in the 1920's and carried out duties as voluntary director of traffic. Not a task which anyone would want to do today! The whitewashed cottage was built in the early 1820's when the Hexham Turnpike Trust began constructing a new turnpike between Corbridge and Heddon on the Wall. The work involved building several new lengths of road linking improved sections of the existing highway where practicable. Nearly two miles of new highway were constructed between Horsley and Heddon, and routed just north of where Holeyn Hall was later built in 1853; this road is the present B3528. The Act of 1820 which authorised construction of the road set tolls of 6d (2.5p) for a horse and carriage, 2d (0.8p) for a horse, ass or beast of burden and 6d (2.5p) for a score of cattle or oxen. During the 1870's the turnpike system was abolished and in January 1877 the toll-houses belonging to the Hexham Turnpike Trust was sold. The Holeyn Hall Toll-House was bought for £40 by E.U. Blackett. Its position on the north-east corner of the crossroads made it an increasing traffic hazard and it was demolished in the late 1920's. Harry MacDowell moved into one of the three terraced houses on the opposite corner of the crossroads.

Back Cover: *Old Locomotive Engine, Wylam Colliery –* by T.H. Hair 1843.

One of the two water colours of Wylam Colliery by Thomas Hair. This view conveys an accurate and dramatic impression of one of the early Wylam locomotives at work on the waggonway (see also pages 7, 34 and 35).

SUBSCRIBERS

Mark Aldridge
Richard and Lawna Allen
Miss Dawn Appleby
William John Appleby
Grace Atkinson
Winifred Ayton
The Baker Family
Beryl Balls
Alastair Balls
David and Adéle Barer
Mr and Mrs G.E. Barker
The Bates Family
Mrs Elizabeth Beaton
Edna Beattie
Mr and Mrs. N.J.T. Bell
John and Helen Bennett
Holly, Verity, Liam and Ailsa
Ann Beresford
The Bergstrand Family
The Beswick-Maddocks Family
Brian Bishop
Alexandra India Blenkley
W.H. Bradley
D. Bradley
Sheila Bradley
Christopher, Carolyn and Lewis Brass
The Brewis Family
Barbara, Rebecca and Matthew Brooks
The Broomfield Family
Dr Ann K. Brough
Dr William Brough
David Buglass
Mr and Mrs W. Burn
Pam and Les Burns
David and Anne Cant
Mr and Mrs Ian Carr
Mrs Thelma Cass
David and Brenda Charlton
Cicely Chetwood and Peter Dodman
Marjorie Coburn
Ray and Jenifer Cole
The Collerton Family
Alan and Dorothy Conley and Family
Anne Cookson
Jim and Pauline Coulson
David J. Craven
John and Angela Craven
Walter and Enid Crawford
Peter and Terry Crichton
The Currie Family
The Doughty Family
Patrick and Dorothy Eavis
Mr and Mrs R. Eccleston
Margaret and Tony Evans
Michael and Susan Ewart
Ros and Arnold Fairless and Family
Foss and Frances Fairnell
Jessica and Aimee Fenwick
Andy and Freda Ferguson
Rev. R. Firth and Mrs Joyce M. Firth
John and Jean Firth and Family
Peter and Alison Fisher
Sarah and Olwyn Fittes
The Fulthorpe Family
Miss Ann Fulton
The Furniss Family
Michael and Jean Gibbney
Maureen and Derek Gillis
John P. and Frances E. Gilmore
The Graham Family
Irene Greig and Family
Bob and Gladys Greenley
John and Hazel Haggith
Mr and Mrs C.A. Haigh
Noel and Anne Hair
Douglas and Sheila Hamilton
The Hardwick Family
Joseph and Freda Hardy
Charles and Penny Harrison
Maurice and Gillian Harvey
Dorothy Hasler
Rob and Daphne Helm
M., A., P. and L. Henderson
Norman and Winnie Henderson
The Hendrick Family
Beryl and Ken Hill
Edward, Brenda and Daron Hodgson
Mike and Susie Holden
George and Joyce Howe
Violet Humphries
Leslie and Elizabeth Hunter
Stephen and Jean Huxley
Marjorie and Peter Isaac
C. and P.M. Jackson
The Jacobson Family
Diana Jervis-Read
Valerie Jervis-Read
Tom Jesson
Anna Jesson
Mike and Pam Johnson
Mr and Mrs R. Johnston
Allan and Norma Jones
Enid Jones and Family
Ian Jones
Vikki Jones
John and Kay Joures
Doreen and Ernie Joy
Bill and Thelma Kitson
Julia and Roy Koerner

Jean and Brian Laing
The Lamb Family
William and Margaret Leadbitter
Mrs Dora Leathard
Ashley and Megan Lidgate
Sheila and Robin Lindsay
C.N. and J.A. Linfoot and Family
Frank G. Littlewood
The Long Family
Colin, Juliet and Frazer Lonie
Percy and Mary Lovell
Lilian Luscombe
Bobbie Joy and Michael Lyster
The McKegney Family
Mr S.J. McKenna
Arthur and Betty McKenzie
Mr and Mrs T.M. Martin
Mr and Mrs L.W. Mew
Elaine and Peter Miller
Ian, Bruce and Faye Miller
The Minnikin Family
Tony and Margaret Mitcham
Harold Mitchell
Robert, Lucy, Ruth and Lydie Monroe
Ken and Joan Murphy
Alec and Kathleen Murray
Allan Murray
Jane Murray
Kay and Paul Myerscough
Mr D.L. and Mrs S. Nicholson
John D. Nicholson

William J. Nicholson
W.L. and M.H. Nixon
Mr and Mrs T.S. Oakley
The Oliver Family
Daniel and Katharine Parker
Fred and Lorraine Parker
Gill and Rob Patterson and Family
June Pattinson
Davina Paverd (New Zealand)
Lynne and David Petrie
Mr and Mrs Sam Phillips
Mr and Mrs I.R. Piette
Dr and Mrs A.C. Piette
Derek, Rosemary and Imogen Proud
Lola Proud and Charles
Dr, Mrs, Anne and David Pullen
Dorothy and Sam Rae
Adrian and Alison Rees and Family
C., R., Z. and E. Ritson
Jim and Brenda Robinson
Mr and Mrs N.R. Robson
Austin and Pat Rubery
Mrs Rosaleen Rutherford
Margaret M. Sanders
Peter and Alison Scott
Les and Marjorie Siddle
Malcolm and Ann Simpson
Gerry and Jenny Slater
Glen and David Smith
Jack and Connie Smith
Howard Smith

Pete, Viv, David and Helen Smith
Ruth and Colin Smith
Elizabeth E. Stephenson
April Stephenson
Peter and Geraldine Tayler
Stephen and Julie Telford
Jonathan T. Telford
J.R. and L. Thompson
The Tomlin Family
C.H. and I.T. Turnbull
Geoffrey and Audrey Turnbull
Dr G.M. Tyce (née Sidebottom)
Evie and Colin Tyson
Bill and Norma Walton
Rob and Val Wanless
The Warren Family
Sue White and Jack Foord
David and Alison Wilkinson
Edna Wilkinson
Joy and David Willday
John and Shirley Williams
Mr and Mrs A. Wilson
Mr John F. Wilson
Graham and Evelyn Wilson
Crian and Sandra Wilson
Linton and Nicola Wilson
The Wray Family
Mr and Mrs A.G.P. Wright
Ian and Shirley Wright
Joyce Wynn
Bill and Babs Yielder